Fragrant Blossoms

Denise S. P. O'Neale

Xulon Press

Xulon Press
2301 Lucien Way #415
Maitland, FL 32751
407.339.4217
www.xulonpress.com

© 2018 by Denise S. P. O'Neale

All rights reserved solely by the author. The author guarantees all contents are original and do not infringe upon the legal rights of any other person or work. No part of this book may be reproduced in any form without the permission of the author. The views expressed in this book are not necessarily those of the publisher.

Unless otherwise indicated, Scripture quotations taken from the King James Version (KJV)–public domain.

Printed in the United States of America.

ISBN-13: 978-1-54560-766-4

The Goldsmith And The Metal

The Goldsmith hammers on the metal, beats it very sore
Upon the anvil of His will, can it take any more?

He puts it in the fire to purge and purify
For the Goldsmith has one thought in mind, "I need to sanctify"

He puts it in the water to cool the raging heat
And looks it over just to see if the metal's meet

There is a flaw and then once more the Hammer and the Anvil
Begin their cruel work again, it must bend to His will

The fire and the water do their cleansing work again
Till metal comes forth pure as gold, it was worth the pain

Your Test Is Over

Don't give up the fight, 'twill all be over in a while
Believe the Word He's promised, keep on trusting
with a smile
Your blessings will rain down upon you, sweeping
o'er your head
You'll be so glad you followed humbly everywhere He led

Your trials seemed so long and hard, you wondered if
you'd pass
You kept your eyes upon Him, all your cares upon Him cast
Amidst the fears and anxious thoughts, you trusted
in His Word
And knew it won't be long before you'd see the blessed Lord

He came so gently and He spoke with words so
kind and true
Did I not say that if you sought Me, I would come to you?
Because you took delight in Me and praised Me in
your storm
Your prayers have all been answered, now receive from My
strong arm

You Decide

So many people are wandering along
With no thought of the way they take
Carelessly moving in step with the throng
And no eternal decisions they make

"Eat, drink and be merry" the quote of the day
Our friends are all here, what's the deal
Life's meant for living, come out and play
While the enemy, your soul waits to steal

You're facing eternity now, all alone
No friends or acquaintance can save
You rejected the One who sits on the throne
And in horror you're facing the grave

Dear friend, if you're living in sin's awful strife
Sin pays its wages in death
Jesus is waiting to give you new life
Choose Him and not this world's wealth

Why Do We Pretend?

Why do we pretend
Is it to show what we are not
Like Pharisees and Sadducees
To gain the highest spot

Why do we pretend
Is it to hide our feelings true
To have complete control
O'er everything we say and do

Why do we pretend
And act as thought we love our brothers
Purporting gifts, we don't possess
Yet hating one another

The heart of God is true
And in His Word no lie is found
Let yea be yea and nay be nay
Let no pretense abound

Wasted Faith

The time I spent in wondering
What will tomorrow bring
I could have spent down on my knees
Before my Lord in praise

The time I spent in wondering
What people thought of me
I could have spent in God's true Word
To know He cares for me

The time I spent in wondering
Of housing, clothes and food
I'd know He feeds the sparrow
And He'll fill my mouth with good

The wasted time, the wasted years
In fears and doubts so great
My faith could've been much stronger
But thank God it's not too late

A Walk In The Trial Side

I've been on the mountain
Where the sun shined warm and bright
I've been in the valley
Where it seemed no end's in sight

I looked for a kind engaging smile
In the face of one called friend
I looked away discouraged
Wondering when will this all end

The road was long and winding
Rocks and hills, they paved the way
Twists and turns, dark dreary nights
Till I heard His sweet voice say

Look unto Me, look to the hills
From whence your help doth come
Take my hand, don't fret or fear
I'll take you safely home

Though tests and trials come your way
Take courage and be bold
Enduring the Refiner's fire
Will bring forth purest gold

Walk Me Throught It

"Come up hither" the Voice did say
Draw closer, closer now
Separate yourself from thing familiar
Full surrender I call for now

Father, mother, sister, brother
Do you love Me more than these?
Come after Me, deny world's treasures
These gods you can't appease

Though long and winding the road may seem
Return not unto sin
He that endureth to the end
A crown of life shall win

And when at last the journey's ended
Heaven's glory is now in view
You'll stand amazed knowing what I meant
When I said "I make all things new"

Visions

What is this I see
Appearing right in front of me?
Beholding things I cannot touch
Not understanding very much

The pictures aren't very clear
I rub my eyes and I draw near
Is this a dream? Are these things so?
Please dear Lord, I need to know

I show you things within My church
Things to which I gave no birth
They're declaring things I did not say
And souls die in their sinful way

Upon my knees I fall and cry
Dear Lord, your power our lives deny
Have mercy and forgive oh Lord
And help us live Your Holy Word

"A new thing" I declare to you
Another vision's now in view
A church triumphant now I see
Marching on to victory

To Soar Like An Eagle

They that wait upon the Lord
Shall mount on eagle's wings
They'll run and not grow weary
They shall walk and not grow faint

He giveth power to the faint
And to those who have no might
Their strength He keeps increasing
Soon they'll spread their wings in flight

Soaring t'ward the clear blue sky
They mount with strength and grace
High against the adverse winds
They find their destined place

He fills my mouth with good
So that my youth's renewed like eagle's
I'll bless my Lord forever
And find pleasure in His temple

The Silent Call

He called me from the place I knew
Into a path unknown
It felt so strange, I knew not how
To go or where to turn

I listened for His tender voice
To tell me where to go
He did not speak, remained so still
Speak Lord, I need to know

"Come after Me" He seemed to say
"Pursue My heart so kind
All heaven is within your reach
Seek Me and you will find"

The Prophets Cry

Prophesy to the nations
Sound out the alarm
Call for true repentance
Turn from sin's dread harm

Send for cunning women
To wail and intercede
Between the porch and altar
Fall down, for your souls plead

"Come now and let us reason
Together" saith the Lord
"Although your sins be scarlet
I'll make them white as snow"

Revival's in the nation
It's spreading o'er the world
March on to certain victory
Christ's banner is unfurled

The enemy is vanquished
We've conquered every foe
He's made us more than conquerors
Defeat we'll no more know

Peace has finally come now
To the new Jerusalem
The war is finally over
We've lain our weapons down

The Joy Of Knowing

Make me to know the utmost joy
In serving You each day
May the passion never fade
As I walk the pilgrim's way

The pathway of the just, I'm told
Is like the brightest light
That shines unto the perfect day
And precious is the sight

And when with humble heart I say
Thank You for loving me
Your joy has been my strength for years
Your faithfulness I see

Oh the joy of knowing you
Your presence is so sweet
Your fragrance fills me with pure life
I'm forever at Your feet

Teach Me Lord To Listen

Teach me Lord to listen, hearing every word You say
You are not confusing in responding when I pray
Voices all around me saying this and saying that
But You bring such calm repose and that Lord is a fact

Moving in Your ordained will, is never quite that easy
I can miss Your next directive, when I get quite busy
But if I still myself enough and let Your peace control
Nothing anyone may say, will move my trusting soul

"I need to run, I need to do," the statements of today
Will take me from the path that's right and then so far away
Because I chose to move in flesh, I miss His blessed will
If only I had listened Lord, if only I stood still

Prophets, they will prophesy, saying it's from You
And the question comes to mind, "Is this utterance true?".
If we'd only listen twice as much as we do speak
Then the church of Jesus Christ will not be so weak

So teach me Lord to listen closely, he that hath an ear
Will hear a still small voice directing, "Go and do not fear"
Stepping out in faith believing, walking in His Word
Will never, ever steer me wrong, I'm so glad I heard

Song Of The Barren

Sing oh barren woman
Thou who didst not bear
Break forth into singing
You shall have an heir

You're pregnant with a promise
'Twas given long ago
By One who set His heart on you
The One who loves you so

A prophet to the nations
Is planted in your womb
With words of life and power
Given by the Holy One

Enlarge your tents and borders
Make room and do not spare
For you shall bear more children
Than the married woman dared

The empty years are over
The years of grief and pain
New life in you is growing
Forget your youthful shame

Push! Oh barren woman
Push! Do not abort
Travailing will be over
Your promise you'll bring forth

Your barren years are ended
The emptiness is passed
Tears of joy are flowing
You're holding your promise at last

Shhhhh!

Study to be quiet, hold your tongue and you will find
There is no confusion, there is peace that's so sublime

He who beareth tales revealeth secrets without fear
Imparting wounds so deep and sore, it's hard for one to bear

Study to be quiet and all gossiping will end
Keep a secret, pray and you will win a trusting friend

You who judge another, are you guilty of same sin?
Or have you taken time to search your own self deep within

A soul is kept from troubles when he keeps his mouth
and tongue
So watch and pray from day to day, you never will go wrong

Rhapsodies From Heaven

What is this faint sound I hear?
Gently falling on my ear
It's a note of sweet refrain
And my heart cannot contain

I sing glory, Hallelujah!
Blessed Saviour so divine
You who reign in might and power
Come and fill this heart of mine

Holy, Holy is the Lord
Pure and righteous are His words
Fill this temple with Your Love
Rest upon us Heavenly Dove

Choirs join the sweet refrain
For the heavens can't contain
The rhapsodies around the throne
They bow before the Holy One

Blessed song of wondrous beauty
Rose of Sharon, fragrant, sweet
We will cast our crowns before You
And ever more sit at Your feet

Press On Dear Ones

Press on dear ones, it won't be long
Press on dear ones, sing Zion's song
Press on, press on though hard the way
Press on into a brand new day

With winding roads and rough, steep hills
The Voice behind keeps whisp'ring still
"Press on, I'm here, you're not alone,
Press on, your journey's almost done"

And when it seems all hope is gone
When the long, hard day is almost done
Press on dear ones, be strong, don't fail
Ere long, you'll be beyond the veil

Panting After God

As the deer panteth after cool and running water
So my soul longeth after Thee
To drink from Living Waters ever flowing, ever free
Quench my thirst and be a well inside of me

Drinking from the well of Living Water
Well of waters boundless and so free
Flow in me that I may know Your Love unceasing
Then flow out that others may be free

See the streams gently rippling o'er the rock to valleys
Babbling brooks whispering gleefully
The shepherd brings His flock to drink from cool and living waters
Then He feeds with bread from heaven prepared for me

Painful Victory

Her past was filled with memories that haunted
through the years
Years of hurt, years of pain, always filled with tears

Her gentle smile and tender voice, belied the bitter pain
She always had a gentle word and works that weren't in vain

"I do not mind, I'll help' she'd say, "what would you
have me do?
I will be there, I'll always share, I'll stay till work is through"

She's home alone, the darkness falls, then comes those
demons sore
Taunting and condemning, screaming "You will never soar!"

Her Saviour came with gentle love and said "I always cared,
I never held your past against you, I was always near"

"My thoughts toward you were always kind, My plans for
you were good
Your pain could've well been over, if upon My Word
you stood"

She looked toward the sky and for the first time saw the rays
And understood that vict'ry will be hers not many days

She's walking in dominion as the righteousness of God
Her past is well behind her, now her feet with
peace are shod

Dear daughter, do not waste your life like me, in
tears of sorrow
Know your future's bright and face with courage
your tomorrow

Creation's Symphony

Some days are just as lovely as a fragrant rose in bloom
Some nights are just as warm and lilting as a merry tune
And sometimes when my heart is sad, I look toward the sky
And oh the joy when I remember, Someone reigns on high

The heavens speak His glory and the earth replies, it seems
The sea-waves roar and echoes o'er the mountains, dales and streams
The thunder claps, the lightning strikes and the trees all sway in praise
The moon, the stars, the sun hang high, all glorious night and day

United by the Conductor, they make so many sounds
They move in many different ways and the melody resounds
Throughout the universe they move and the sweet refrain is heard
Creation's symphony crescendos, without a single word

Breathe On Me

Breathe on me oh breath of God
Fill me with Thy Word
Lift me up above the storm
Hold me fast, keep safe from harm
Breathe on me oh breath of God
Holy Lord

Lead me through the valleys low
In the darkness help me know
You are with me all the way
Watching o'er me day by day
Lead me through the valleys low
Holy Lord

Help me scale the mountains tall
Hold me up, lest I fall
Bounding up with feet like hinds'
Upon my high place I will find
That I've scaled the mountains tall
Holy Lord

When at last I see Thy face
Knowing then 'twas by Thy grace
That I stand on heaven's shore
There to praise Thee evermore
Oh what joy to see Thy face
Blessed Lord

Holy Intimacy

Hold me Lord, embrace me Lord
I need Your tender touch
Draw me closer to Your side
I love You oh so much

Your presence sets my heart aflame
Your fragrance fills the room
Your gentle Voice brings wondrous calm
Dispelling fear and gloom

Just stay right here and speak to me
Linger for a while
Speak words of love in tender tones
Charm me with Your smile

The consummation of God's love
Will bring contentment sweet
I'm intimate with One in worship
What glorious, blessed retreat

I lay me down in peace and sleep
Delighted with my Love
My deepest longings I will know
When I'm kissed by God above

In Praise And Thanksgiving

Come let us sing unto the Lord
Let's make a joyful noise
Lifting hands that's pure and holy
Giving praise to Him who's worthy
Gather round the throne

Praise Him on the instruments
Magnify His name
Holy, Holy, God Almighty
Welcome oh Shekinah Glory
Fall on us we pray

Around the altar, hearts are joyful
Dancing with delight
For great things which You have done
And for Your Beloved Son
We thank You, day and night

Ichabod's Reprieve

The glory has departed
The Light no longer shines
The water has abated
The church has crossed the lines

What's the use in birthing?
If Glory is not there
What's the use of mirthing?
If His presence is not near

We long to see Your glory
Return to us we pray
We'll show forth Your perfection
We'll do whate'er You say

We'll fall in sackcloth, ashes
We'll cry, we'll weep and mourn
Repentance and contrition
Our faces now adorn

I'm stripped and bare before You
The Light now shines in me
The Glory has returned now
I'm filled, I'm whole and I'm free

I Am Compelled

I am compelled to look beyond the fancies of today
To look upon my Saviour and His Holy will obey
I am compelled to walk in love, as Jesus first loved me
And let His light so shine until in Him I'm whole and free

Deny me not the visions clear, nor withhold Your
Spirit's power
I need Thee, how I need Thee in my life each passing hour
Deny me not Thy presence for without Thee I won't live
My life, my love, my heart, my all without reserve to
Thee I give

Charmed By Deceit

Deceit came with subtlety
With warm and gentle smile
The caring tone and loving voice
Belied the wretched guile

"My name is Christian too" he said
And tears came streaming down
My heart was glad and I rejoiced
But no truth in him was found

"Strongman" entered my domain
And slowly took control
Soon I was running, bound by fear
My home was his stronghold

I sought a friend who knew the Lord
Who understood my pain
We prayed and broke deceiver's hold
My strength I did regain

With new found faith and authority
I faced that demon sore
And took back what he stole from me
Deceiver lives here no more

Can You Believe?

Said I not to thee
If you'd believe Me you would see
The Glory of the Father
In your life revealed through Me?

Why do you choose to doubt
When I have promised in My Word
Your needs will be supplied
I'm not like man, I am the Lord

I conquered death and hell
I rose with healing in my wings
All power is given to Me
In heaven and earth, I'm king of kings

Said I not to thee
If you believe Me you would see?
Let not your heart be troubled
Bring all your anxious cares to Me

The battle's Mine
I am the Captain of the heavenly host
Take courage, do not faint
The victory's yours when needed most

Can I Be Real With You?

Can I be real with you
When I am not what I should be?
Can I be real with you
If Christ in me, you cannot see?

Can I be real with you
When tempted by the devil sore?
And give in to deep passions
Will I see you never more?

Can I be real with you
When attitude is not quite right?
When tempers flare, will you dare
To stand by me and fight?

Can I be Real with you
Dear friend, or will you walk away
Can I be true to me
And know no matter what, you'd stay?

There is a friend I know
Who sticks much closer than a brother
Are just like Him
Or do you condemn like the others"

If I can be real with you
If I can share my heart
Then you would prove a friend that's true
A friend who won't depart

Belover El Shaddai

His grace is sufficient, His love does make me strong
In Him I find sweet peace and joy, in me He placed a song

I'll love Him truly all my days and never turn aside
He'll guide my footsteps all the way, in His Light I'll abide

Sweet gentle Shepherd, lead me on, don't leave me
nor forsake
Feed me in Your pastures green, with gentleness and grace

I hunger for Your Righteousness, I thirst for living waters
That flow from heavenly streams above, and fill my heart
with laughter

My strength's renewed, I am refreshed, and a well now
springs within
Oh may it never cease in me, these waters gushing free

No Room

No room in the inn for the Christ Child
No room, but a manger stall
Was all that the inn-keeper offered
To the One who was born to save all

No room in your heart for the King of kings
For it's ruled by this world's goodly fares
And the god of this world sits enthroned within
While your heart by its sovereign is snared

No room in your life for the Master
No room, it has set its own course
Your future's all mapped out, there is no time
For repentance, not even the cross

No room for the gospel of Jesus
No room to begin life anew
"I mastered my fate, I captained my soul"
Now before Him you stand who is true

No room in the heavenly Kingdom of God
No room, you rejected My Son
Depart from Me, you missed your last chance
To embrace what the Saviour has done

No Other Love

His caresses are gentler than a summer breeze
I'm warm in His embrace
His kiss is sweet, His arms are strong
I'm captured in His Love

He whispered gentle, loving words
He drew me close to Him
We spoke of many wondrous things
I, to my Love now cling

I yield, I yield, My Love I yield
To passions sweet and strong
To tender love that warms my heart
That climaxes in song

I'm satisfied, I want no other
No one e'er loved me so
Perfect Lover, Dearest Friend
One heartbeat till the end

My Shepherd, His Sheep

The Lord is my Shepherd
He cares for His sheep
He feeds in green pastures
He safely doth keep

Beside the still waters
So cool and refreshing
He leads me to drink
My thirst He is quenching

The Lord is my Shepherd
In Him there's no lack
My need He supplies
He won't take His Word back

A table's prepared
In the midst of my foes
Delicious, rich dainties
On me He bestows

Goodness and Mercy
My partners for life
Have followed me closely
With peace not in strife

And when through dark valleys
Death's shadows I face
My heart will not fear
For I'm saved by His grace

My Lord And I

There is a place where I can go
A place where heavenly breezes blow
A place where I can take it slow
Communing with my Lord

It is a place of quiet rest
That special place I love the best
It's where I know I'm truly blessed
Walking with my Lord

No other friend can come with me
It's where my Lord and I can be
In sweet communion glad and free
I'm feasting with my Lord

My Heart's Desire

I want You Lord above all else
I love You more than life
I'm forsaking all to follow You:
This world and all its strife

If I should turn and walk away
To whom Lord shall I go?
You possess the Words of life
You washed me white as snow

Each day with You grows sweeter Lord
Embrace me in Your Love
Be Thou my breath, my life, my joy
Till I see Your face above

Love's Greatest Gift

Love's greatest gift came down to earth
In a humble manger stall
Gently wrapped in swaddling clothes
Then came the angels' call

For unto you is born this day
A Saviour, Christ the Lord
He shall save you from your sins
According to His Word

The shepherds hastened to the place
Where the King of Glory lay
With bleating sheep and oxen lowing
Upon a bed of hay

The wise men from the East, we're told
Came following the star
That led to Bethlehem that night
They had traveled very far

Gold and Frankincense and Myrrh
Their precious gifts did bring
To welcome Him Whom God did send
The Everlasting King

And still today we look for Him
Who's coming once again
Not as a babe in Bethlehem
But as King of kings to reign

It's All About Me

Lo I come in the volume of the Book
It's written concerning Me
I came to do My Father's will
I require no lees of thee

Just as My Father and I are one
Let Me be one with thee
No one can pluck from My strong hand
Those that were given Me

Go ye into all the world
And tell the Gospel's truth
From your hometown to the nation 'round
The world and don't dilute

Souls are at stake, so don't delay
My Word you must declare
So keep in mind, all that you speak
Concerns no one but Me

Don't Lose Sight Of The Cross

Don't lose sight of the cross
It's where new life begins
Don't lose sight of the cross
Or the price for your sins

A Saviour came down
With one purpose in mind
To die for us all
Who by darkness was blind

Don't lose sight of the cross
Or the blood that was shed
He laid his life down
He died in our stead

His Love held Him there
What great sacrifice
Our sins on Him laid
He's the ultimate price

In sorrow he died
Triumphant He rose
Over death and the grave
The saints' final foes

So never forget where your new life began
Never forget, He was God's perfect plan
Forget not the day He called you His own
Now worship the One who sits on heavens throne

Glorious Tidings

Glory to God in the highest
Peace and good will on the earth
For unto you is born this day
A Saviour of lowly birth

Tell the glad tidings to all men
Tell of God's gift to them all
Tell them of wondrous salvation
If on the Lord they will call

Sing for Christ Jesus is come from heaven
Dance and rejoice with great joy
Christmas is here and we'll celebrate
With all the girls and the boys

Glory to God in the highest
Marvelous gift to us giv'n
Jesus the Saviour has come to earth
Humbly in Bethlehem

You Are

You are real, You are true
There's no other Lord like You
You bring joy and love divine
And You're mine
You're from age to age the same
Lord I bless Your holy name
Strength and honour's due to You
I love You

Come Holy Fount, spring up within
To everlasting life that's free from sin
Restore, refresh, revive, renew my soul
That makes me whole

Miriam's Song

I will dance, I will sing
I will play before my King
I will bow and I'll adore
Praise Jehovah o'er and o'er

He hath brought us out with a mighty hand
Rescued us from our enemies
Bound, afflicted sore in Egypt's land
Through the mighty seas

Let's rejoice in our God
Death passed o'er us through the blood
He who led us through the sea
Pharaoh's army we'll no more see

I'll delight in the Lord
In His presence and in His Word
Jesus Christ is His name
Yesterday, today, forever the same

Midnight's Song

Give me a song to sing at midnight
Give me a song to sing at day
A song that breaks the powers of darkness
And brings men to a brand new day

Give me a word to speak to someone
A word that sets the captives free
Proclaiming liberty and victory
By the anointing that's on me

Oh may I be a living witness
Constrained by God's redeeming love
I want to be Your humble servant
Descend upon me Heavenly Dove

Give me a song to sing at midnight
Give me a word to speak at day
A prayer that brings complete deliverance
Until You call me home someday

Hallelujah! Hallelujah!

Hallelujah, hallelujah, hallelujah to the King of kings
Hallelujah, hallelujah, hallelujah to the Lord of lords
He hath built us upon a firm foundation
Hallelujah, hallelujah
He established us by His might power
Hallelujah, hallelujah

Praise Of A Psalmist

Come into His gates with thanksgiving
Enter in His courts with praise
Worship Him because He is worthy
Give Him glory all my days

Lord I bow at Your feet
In Your presence so sweet
I embrace You and hold You so near
Angels dance round Your throne
Singing Holy One
To the Ancient of days, eternal praise

I will bless the Lord at all times
His praise shall always be in my mouth
Oh my soul shall boast in You Lord
Every ear shall hear and be glad
I will bless Your name
Ever more You're the same
I rejoice in the work of our hands
Lord it's You I adore
Like an eagle I soar
In Your presence on wings of praise

Changes

Come happy children, laugh and play
This is the day that I have made
I am the Truth, the Life, the Way
Come children play

Your life was filled with misery
My glory you couldn't really see
But now be glad, be whole and free
Come bow the knee

My praise was not your covering
Though I bore you on eagle's wings
I set you free from suffering
So sing children sing

I call you Mine, I am your God
I placed you on this earthly sod
To be a witness of My Word
Now bear the Sword

Unity Never Hurts

Life is meant for living
We were meant to be
Why do we keep striving?
Why are we not free?

We are so divided
Split in many ways
We need to be reminded
Who made us all one day

The Master, our Creator
Made us as He pleased
With many different colours
And languages and needs

He fashioned and He formed us
To be His jewels rare
But we have lost our focus
We're loaded down with care

If we could love our brother
If we would be so kind
To care for one another
And let true love be blind

Our course in life may take us
To many different lands
Let's treasure what is precious
Extend a helping hand

So let us come together
In unity, let's stand
Come sisters, come my brothers
Let's walk hand in hand

I Do Love You

You are my everything
Of You alone I sing
You are my God and King
And I love you

You are my sole desire
You set my soul on fire
Of you I'll never tire
"Cause I love You

You are my dearest Friend
This love will never end
On You I can depend
How I love You

And when I leave this place
Soaring through time and space
I'll finally see Your face
To e'er love You

Sweet Adonai

Adonai, sweet Adonai
We praise Your name, we lift You high
We raise our voices to the sky
Sweet Adonai

Adonai, sweet Adonai
Your presence we cannot deny
For You are true, You cannot lie
Sweet Adonai

Adonai, sweet Adonai
Without You we would surely die
Oh come to us, don't pass us by
Sweet Adonai

Adonai, dear Adonai
Hear us as we humbly cry
We love You deeply, draw us nigh
Dear Adonai

Reverential Worship

He's near, he's near, the Lord is near
Oh taste and see He's good
His name we speak with holy fear
And serve Him as we should

He's altogether beautiful
He's more than words can say
I love Him, He's so wonderful
I'll worship Him always

He's Adonai, my Adonai
He's Yahweh just and true
No other God can satisfy
My heart, I do love You

Oh Rose of Sharon, fragrant, sweet
Your presence I embrace
I bow in reverence at Your feet
And long to see Your face

Positioned To Prosper

I'm positioned to prosper
Beyond wealth or means
I'm positioned to prosper
I've seen it in dreams

From the pit to the palace
From servant to king
I'm here by Your grace
A success in the making

From the sheepfold to the throne
Anointed to reign
Though hunted and alone
I will worship His name

I'm positioned to prosper
In abundance I walk
Positioned to prosper
Hear me when I talk

From a captive to queen
I have the King's favour
I'm fragrant and clean
My new life I now savour

From Moab to Bethlehem
A widow was I
I gleaned among men
Then I caught my Lord's eye

Down to the threshing floor
He covered me there
Now lacking no more
I am His without fear

I'm positioned to prosper
I'm destined to rise
By faith now I soar
Beyond cloudless blue skies

Chosen Before Birth

He chose me before the world began
He chose me and formed in me His perfect plan
A vessel of honour, sanctified, holy
A pattern unique, I belong to Him only

He put in me words to speak to the nations
My destiny forged, not by man's mental notions
And although my life did not match His requirements
He knew that one day I'd defy every argument

He called me everything good that I was not
Thought tainted and vile, He removed every blot
A daughter of righteousness He called me
Beloved and favoured, how could this be?

He knew me and called from eternity past
He placed in me power that forever would last
And now by His grace, forgiven I stand
Predestined and led by His almighty hand

Remember

Oh the precious name of Jesus
Is so wonderful to me
Brings me peace and brings me comfort
When the way I cannot see

When life's trials overwhelm me
When my tears flow like a flood
Fears and torments come so painful
I'm reminded, trust God's Word

When I question my salvation
And dear Abba's love for me
He gently comes and He reminds me
We belong, don't fail to see

See My love for you dear daughter
See My hand upholding you
You're surrounded by my presence
You're coming out, though going through

There's an end to this rough pathway
Praise Me through your heartfelt pain
Trust Me in your darkest hours
Soon I'll come like cool, fresh rain

Rains are flowing ever freely
Downpours like they'll never end
Face uplifted to the heavens
Come dear Lord, revive again

I wrote this poem when I was going through a very difficult time. Money was very low, I could not pay my bills as I ought. Trusting God for deliverance was hard and my body was reacting to all of this with awful pain

I Am Compelled

I am compelled to look beyond the fancies of today
To look upon my Saviour and His holy will obey
I am compelled to walk in love as Jesus first loved me
And let His light so shine until in Him, I'm whole and free

Deny me not the visions clear, nor withhold Your spirit's power
I need Thee, how I need Thee in my life each passing hour
Deny me not Thy presence for without Thee I won't live
My life, my love, my heart, my all without reserve to thee I give

Tuning In

I'm tuning in to Holy Spirit
Tuning in to Living Words
Words of comfort and instruction
As I yield to my true Lord

I am listening more closely
As I waken to His voice
He alone knows how to touch me
He, my one true faithful choice

There's a path that lies before me
Leading me to realms unknown
Realms of glory, now I see it
I possess what once was shown

Bind Me

Written by Denise O'Neale – 7/14/16

Bind me to Your altar as a living sacrifice
Purge me with Your hyssop, wash me clean
Break me now, oh Potter, I am marred and so undone
Get into those parts to me unseen

Lord I am so weary of the weaknesses within
Tired of the secret sins I do
Help me scale these hurdles, help me climb these mountains tall
Help me trust in Him who's tried and true

When will this be over, I can hear my spirit cry
Trials seem to come on every hand
At times dear Lord I falter and when I doubt, I fall
But clothed in Your great armor I can stand

This won't last forever, it will all come to an end
Victory is just around the bend
I'll hold on to Your promises and trust You will come through
For that is what You are, it's what You do

On Your brazen altar I surrender all of me
Dead to sin, but living whole and free
Out of the ashes you have made me beautiful within
Seated in the heavenly place with Christ, I win

After reading L. B. Cowman's "Streams in the Desert" and Psalm 118:27 on 7/14/16 during my devotions.

Be Encouraged

Whenever you begin to feel like life has let you down
Do not be discouraged, you're a jewel in My crown

When others seem to pass you by and not acknowledge you.
Remember you are in My heart, to you I'm always true

I formed you with a plan in mind and it will come to pass
So trust Me in your darkest hour, these trying times
won't last

You are precious, you are valued despite what others say
My love for you will never change until eternal day

I'm your supply, and your best friend, I am a faithful Lover
So please do not forget, I am in love with you forever

His Presence My Comfort

In the presence of the Lord there is Peace
In the presence of the Lord there is rest
There is grace, there is hope, there is love
There is joy from above
In the presence of the Lord

In the presence of the Lord there is strength
In the presence of the Lord there is comfort
He speaks "Peace be still and know,
I am God, My power I'll show"
In the presence of the Lord

In the presence of the Lord there is Truth
In the presence of the Lord there is mercy
Lord I praise Your holy name
Worship Yahweh unashamed
In the presence of the Lord

Written on 10/26/09 after a let down from a friend

In His Presence

Oh the sweetness of His presence
When with Christ my Lord I am
Finding pleasure in the essence
Of His love that brings great calm

In the splendour of the sunlight
I am basking every day
And sometimes when life brings midnight
I'll not fear, I'll watch and pray

Walking daily with my Saviour
I have blessed, calm repose
Naught from me, my Lord can sever
For He has triumphed o'er His foes

My soul will cling to Him forever
Trusting Him where e'er I be
He'll forsake and leave me never
Till His glorious face I see

I'll Be There To Comfort You

I'll be there to comfort you
To walk with you when skies are blue
Through thunderstorms and monsoon rain
In blissful times and awful pain

Just when you think that I'm not near
I'm closer than you think my dear
Holding you in arms of love
For you're my faithful, gentle dove

Press on through, you're almost there
I'm here, you have no need to fear
Your future's bright, your pathway plain
Soon you'll rise in Me again

My storms were sent to strengthen you
Your roots went deeper, now your view
Has changed to see from eagle's height
Now walk by faith, no more by sight

Purified To Worship

Purify my heart with Your love divine
Set me Lord apart to glorify Your name

Purge me Lord with fire, refine and set aflame
Fill me with desire to magnify Your name

Fill me Lord with praise, my songs to You I'll raise
I'll give You all my days to worship You always

Fit me Lord to serve, equip and set apart
Faithful service You deserve with gentleness of heart

Worship

I came into the Holy place
I heard Him speak with gentle grace
"Come and seek My blessed face
And find sweet rest and peace

Your answers you will surely find
I always have you on My mind
My thoughts t'ward you are always kind
So trust My righteous hand"

Worship, worship and adore
Lord I praise You o'er and o'er
I'll love You more and more
I lay prostrate for You are
The Glorious, Holy One
Shine on me Glorious "Sun"
Now let Your will be done
I worship and adore

Cast upon Me all your cares
Do not worry, doubt or fear
Don't you know I'm always there
To bring you through each trial?
A fresh anointing now I need

To come before and intercede
To love in word, in thought and deed
Your Glory now I see

You Alone Are Worthy

You alone are worthy to receive all glory
You alone are worthy to be praised
We bow down before You
Heaven and earth adore You
You alone are worthy to be praised

Praise Him! Praise Him!
We worship You with holy hands upraised
Praise Him! Praise Him!
You alone are worthy to be praised

I'm In Your Hands

I'm in your hand
To do as You command
I'm in Your hand
Use me Lord

I'm in Your care
My heart shall know no fear
I'm in Your care
Send me Lord

I will not be ashamed
To call upon Your name
Your mighty words to this world I must proclaim
I will go in the power of Your might
For I walk by faith and not by sight

I'm in Your heart
Sweet Wonder don't depart
I'm in Your heart
Love me Lord

It's In The Praise

When it seems odds are against you
And you're baffled many days
You'll not find sweet peace in murmuring
You will find it's in the praise

When like Martha you're encumbered
Laden down with many cares
Do not be frustrated, Christian
Lift your hands and give God praise

Praise can bring down Satan's stronghold
Praise can surely bring you out
Praise will lead you into victory
Come on Christian, you can shout

My Lord And I

There is a place where I can go
A place where heavenly breezes blow
A place where I can take it slow
Communing with my Lord

It is a place of quiet rest
That special place I love the best
It's where I know I'm truly blessed
Walking with my Lord

No other friend can come with me
It's where my Lord and I can be
In sweet communion glad and free
I'm feasting with my Lord

Unity In My Body

I knelt before my Lord today
His presence I desired
Confessing sins, being cleansed within
Praising Him was now required

My body says "I'm feeling tired
I want to go to sleep
It's been a long and dreary day
You time with God will keep

My Soul is saying "sing a song,
Remember things to do
I can't be quiet, it's much too hard
Let's call it quits, we're through"

My spirit's saying "let us soar
Let's go beyond the veil
A new experience with the Lord
We're going to have, don't fail"

I tell my body "Come in line"
My mind, "Get in accord!"
My spirit sings because we three
Are in union with the Lord

Let Us Return

This house was once a hallowed place
Where God was in control
Where reverence marked each sainted face
And God's glory was the goal

The fear of God was on each heart
Blest silence filled the room
God's will, to us, with power impart
And we'd shun hell's dark gloom

But now this is the "Age of Grace"
In stubborn pride we stay
No reverence in this sacred place
And lots of time to play and little time to pray

Our children don't regard the Lord
We never taught them how
While God speaks from His holy Word
We talk and laugh, not bow

The alarm is sounded, there's a call
For values once held dear
"I still demand respect from all
And My name regard with fear

He Knows How To Touch

He knows how to touch you
He won't pervert or defile
There's healing and He will restore
The years, the trust, the smile

For years I thought I'd never want
The touch of mortal man
The walls of pain and shame I built
Would ne'er come down again

The hardness and the anger
Kept potential friends at bay
I was content with solitude
Until one blessed day

A tender, strong and unseen hand
Uprooted years of fears
I screamed in pain and agony
And then flowed cleansing tears

There's healing and there's wholeness
Life and love look brighter now
The perfect touch of Jesus Christ
Is what I did allow

Canaan's Song Of Deliverance

Sing unto the Lord
For He hath triumphed gloriously
Egypt's horse and rider
He hath thrown into the sea

Sing unto the Lord
For He hath saved with mighty hand
The Red Sea He did part
Now we are bound for Canaan Land

Dance and play before Him
With timbrel and harp
Lift one voice in song unto Him
No more slaves are we

Sing unto the Lord
For milk and honey's flowing free
The enemy is vanquished
We have perfect liberty

Worshipful Praise

Well it's alright now
I'm gonna make it somehow
With God on my side
I will abide

'Neath the shadow of Thy wing
Your grace helps me to sing
In perfect harmony
Along with Thee

See my days were cloudy and grey
I thought I'd lost my way
Then You made it clear to me
"I am with thee"

Then I turned my eyes t'ward You
Heaven's glory came in view
Now with thankful heart I praise
You all my days

Blessings and glory and honour now
Worshipping You at Your throne I bow
There's no one else that I treasure more than You
Wonderful, marvelous Lord You are
You are my bright and my Morning Star
My Saviour, my Lord and my precious King
You are my everything
Of You I sing
My praise I bring
You are my everything

Nevertheless, I Still Believe

The course of nature does not flow
The way I always choose
But yet a gentle voice says "Go"
Don't rest upon man's views

The path to Glory is sometimes fraught
With dangers dark and grim
But when I trust Him as I'm taught
My faith will not grow dim

When disappointments come my way
And things don't go as planned
I fall upon my knees and pray
Lord guide me with Your hand

When good friends say "just give it up"
And emotions fluctuate
That gentle voice says "don't give up"
Your God is never late

With a brand new day and brand new sight
I rise to leave once more
The doubts and fears that plague at night
And on wings of faith I soar

Possessing My Future

I'm not my own
I am bought with a price
Not of silver or gold
But with the blood of Jesus Christ

Rest in the Lord
Wait patiently for Him
Fret not yourself
Though your pathway looks dim

You still have a future
There's success up ahead
You've inherited the land
As Joshua 1:3 said

Forget former things
Don't consider the old
I'm making all new
Soon this vision I'll unfold

Be Careful

Be careful who you listen to
Be careful what you hear
The message you're receiving
Will be coming loud and clear

Well meaning, but mis-spoken words
Can damage and do harm
Disturbing blessed confidence
Removing peaceful calm

Guard your heart with diligence
Handle it with care
He who sits on heaven's throne
Is also very near

Listen very carefully
He speaks in gentle tones
That brings sweet comfort in the night
And guides through the unknown

Rest calmly in His precious love
Lean gently on His breast
He's heard and brought you through lean years
Now trust Him for the rest

What Wait Ye For

What wait ye for?
The Master bids you come
Oh don't delay
What wait ye for?
Tomorrow is not promised, you only have today
What wait ye for?
Incessantly He's knocking at your door
Dear friend, don't think he'll knock forevermore
What wait ye for?
When Christ with wondrous treasures for you bring
What wait ye for?
The life, the love, the parties will not last
You've searched so long to fill the void within
Not drugs, nor drinks would satisfy, no sin
Will bring true joy and peace you try to find
Your so-called friend the enemy has made you to
Christ blind
What wait ye for?
On bended knee before the Saviour fall
What wait ye for?
He's waited oh so long to hear you call
Oh wait no more
All angels round the throne of God rejoice
The One you've wanted, needed now
And evermore is your choice

Wind Song

Come gently to me Saviour
Fill me up this very hour
My heart is opened to receive
The reverential shower

The comforter did come and seal
Your Holy truths to me reveal
My soul with heavenly manna feed
Your Love to me is real

Incense of praise to Thee I send
You are such a faithful friend
Your life in me, a perfect blend
Forever to the end

Playful Lord

Come play before Me precious child
In wild abandon play
Come run into My opened arms
And in My presence stay

Come swim in crystal waters cool
Roll in grassy fields
Laugh in joyous, youthful tones
Rest 'Neath shady trees

Talk to Me of life and love
Tell me all your heart
Leave nothing out, remember now
I've known you from the start

Never fear to play before Me
Show Me how you feel
Heaven and earth you're now embracing
I love it when you're real

I'm Still, He's God

Be still and know that I am God
Take courage friend, be bold
The Lord thy God is on thy side
My grace I'll not withhold

Stand still and see me save all round
Dear soul, take calm repose
Though the vision tarries for a time
Its depths I'll soon unfold

I'm walking in the plan of God
My purpose to fulfill
No greater joy can e'er be found
Than in God's perfect will

Standing Strong

When troubles rise from murky deep
And robs the soul of blessed sleep
Tis then we fall on bended knee
And cry, Lord we've no help but Thee

When adverse winds begin to blow
The sea waves roar and billows roll
The Master's voice, commands them cease
And o'er my soul comes wondrous peace

When loved ones strike with brutal force
The hordes of hell must run their course
I'll stand, not sway, with courage, for
This fight's not mine, it is the Lord's

Scarred and wounded, yet I stand
Because the Saviour held my hand
Undefeated, bolder, stronger
I am more than a conqueror

Still I Stand

When the cares of this life overtake me
And the enemy attacks on every hand
When the storms of hell doth assail me
It's then I will take my stand

When praise and worship escape me
And emotions ride high like the tide
When I want to give up because of what I see
I will stand on Your word, I'll abide

When it seems like no one understands me
And friendships appear all too few
I will look to the One who supports me
Who promised to be faithful and true

I will stand though the storm winds are blowing
I will stand though forsaken by all
After counting the cost, I stand knowing
God has got me; He won't let me fall

Enduring Life's Storms

Oh restless child tossed to and fro
By storms and adverse winds that blow
Can you face them with a song?
Assured deliverance won't be long

My daughter, I created you
Aware of all that you'd go through
Through fires, waters, you won't die
Soon you will soar like eagles on high

Dear humble servant, steadfast and strong
Did I not say it won't be long?
You've scaled your mountains, you've got hinds' feet
You're more than a conqueror, Satan's under your feet

And when at last we're face to face
You'll know it was by My grace
That you stood tall like islands' palms
And faced each tempest sure and calm

Mary's Song

My soul doth magnify the Lord
My joyful heart doth sing
For He hath done great things for me
I praise the King of kings

I will dance before the Lord
Clap my hands unto the Lord
For He delivered, by His name
Set me free from sin and shame
I will dance before the Lord
Clap my hands unto the Lord

I stand in awe before the Lord
His presence brings sweet peace
In praise I've found deliverance
His blessings never cease

The evidence of joy divine
Is now my blest abode
His banner over me is Love
I'm walking in His Word

Driven

I'm driven by desires that consume me night and day
Compelled to yield to sinful acts that keep the Lord at bay
When passions burn like white hot heat, I never think to try
To find the way that's marked "Escape," my flesh just
says "comply"

I'm driven by the things I see; I want what I can't own
Pursuing and embracing idols, coveting the unknown
Today my flesh is hungry and it's screaming "Feed me now!"
And without a moment's thought, I to my flesh do
humbly bow

I'm wasted and I'm famished, not content from giving in
The bowels of hell are opened to me, luring me within
Then suddenly in desperation, I cried out to the Lord
Deliverance came and now I'm feasting on His Holy Word

My friend, if you are driven by desires' burning coal
Remember there are angels warring for your precious soul
Make Christ your choice and He will give desires
pure and Holy
That drive you toward His presence, now you're free to love
Him wholly

Give Me You

Give Me your heart, I've given Mine, never falter nor repine
Love Me as I love, don't hold back, say "I'm wholly Thine"

Thine oh Lord, Thine oh Lord
Leaning on Thy Holy Word
Thine oh Lord, Thine oh Lord
I am wholly Thine

Give Me your all, come follow closely, watch Me do exceedingly
Abundant life is yours, just claim it, now come follow Me

Follow Me, follow Me
I in thee, the world must see
Follow Me, follow Me
Thine I'll always be

Oh Come Sweet Spring

The summer sun burns bright above
With subtle warmth of heavenly love
Clear skies of blue and grasses green
The Father's handiwork is seen

The fall, its radiant colours bring
Through leaves of gold I walk and sing
With thankful heart I stop and ponder
On all of nature's natural wonders

The winter's harsh and barren cold
Chills the bones of young and old
And life can, for a moment seem
Devoid of hope that makes me dream

Then comes sweet spring with glorious life
All things are new amid earth's strife
Showers of blessings upon us rain
Then seasons' change begins again

So when it seems like all is lost
And all green things turn to hoar-frost
The best of life is yet to come
For seasons' change is never done

Strange Tests

A strange and awesome test has come
To those who seek to know
The heart and mind of Father God
It's a process painfully slow

A strange and awesome test has come
To break the stoutest heart
Made hard and crusty by sin's pride
Forgiveness to impart

The strangest tests will come to those
Who choose, like Christ, to die
Upon the altar of God's will
And the world's dark ways deny

Blow by blow, the strangest tests
Breaks up the fallow ground
To plant the seeds of Love and Truth
Till Joy and Peace is found

And when the strangest test is done
A new anointing flows
Through yielded vessels pure and clean
Christ's image through us shows

The Path Least Understood

The path of life that's taken
Is as winding as can be
And though sometimes we're shaken
We can walk this path that's free

Many feet have walked in paths
That's filled with sorrows, fears
Other feet have taken paths
Of pain and hurt and tears

There is a path that leads to life
It's filled with hopes and dreams
It is not paved with sin and strife
Nor man's destructive schemes

This winding path of jagged stones
Is paved with glorious Truth
With valleys deep and mountains high
We still bear precious fruit

When closest friends misjudge your words
When faults and flaws deride
It's then I need my precious Lord
To make my doubts subside

The winding path to glory friends
Is paved with so much good
With twists and turns and bumps and bends
It's the path least understood

Oh weary traveler, don't despair
This path will not destroy
It tends to life so do not fear
Don't let your foes annoy

And when at last your journey's done
Misunderstanding's ceased
You did not fail, you've overcome
Now walk on golden streets

Flowing With My Lord

Sometimes I do not understand
The ways and mind of God
Just when I see His mighty hand
Moving all across the land
To bring to pass some blessing grand
He brings hard trials once more

"Just trust My Word" He says to me
"I will not steer you wrong"
And then I move with steps unsure
In the Light that hovers o'er
The path that leads to life and more
He guides me with His love

I do not know what lies ahead
Nor what the future holds
But this one blessed truth I know
When the heavenly breezes blow
It's best that I get in the flow
It'll lead me safely home

I Am Loved

Lovingly He watches o'er me
Tenderly He speaks
All day long He's caring for me
Even when I sleep

Warm and tender His caresses
His embrace is strong
And my hungry soul He blesses
With a lilting song

Fiery, His heated passion
Has consumed my heart
My mind and will He forms and fashions
And His purest thoughts impart

I'll respond to Love unending
His captive I will be
For in this blessed, Holy union
I am whole and free

He Has Dove's Eyes For Me

I love a man I've yet to meet
A man so strong, yet tender, sweet
Who loves the Lord with all his heart
And from his Lord he'll ne'er depart

The man I love walks very tall
Agape love he bears for all
No compromise is found within
And like his Father, he hates sin

He's warm and loving, funny too
A laid-back kind of guy and cool
A family man who will not stray
So fine and beautiful in his way

Warrior, worshipper, lover is he
Magnanimous and he loves me
I am his rib, his perfect fit
And to this man I do commit

He is God's man, he's also mine
Devoted, down-to-earth and divine
He has some faults for he's a man
And for me, he's God's master plan

We are one by God's design
And to my love I now resign
I'll honour him, this man I love
Who's eyes for me are like a dove

Just To Say Thank You

What words can I utter Lord
How can I express
This overwhelming sense of awe
I feel when in Your presence

You overflow me like high tides
I burn with Holy fire
Consuming me so tenderly
Till there's one pure desire

I love You Lord, You know I do
With heart and soul and mind
You alone possess my heart
To other loves I'm blind

How can I thank You Precious Lord?
For great blessings poured on me
A simple thank You is not enough
To say all You mean to me

So Lord I give You all my life
My future's in your hand
I won't look back, I've counted the cost
Now use me as You planned

The Meaning Of Christmas

Born a King of humble birth
God in flesh did come to earth
Angels in the heavens did say
Peace, goodwill to man today
And with glad hearts joyfully
Loving thanks we give to Thee
Worshipping most reverently
That's what Christmas means to me

The Pathway Of Purity

Pursuing the pathway of purity
Is by no way an easy journey
It's fraught with suggestions
Innuendos and temptations
And losses that can't be recovered

Pursuing the pathway of purity
Is lined with delightful frivolity
One compromise made
And one kiss in the shade
Brings the strong urge to go one step farther

Enemies on the pathway of purity
Seek to trap those who walk in naiveté
To taste forbidden sin
By luring them in
To a web that's hard to be broken

Surviving the pathway of purity
Abstaining from hell's immorality
Gains a healthy respect
And a Godly prospect
With no regrets for making right choices

I wrote this poem on 1/6/13, after listening to Lisa Bevere on Family Life Today talk about being invited to speak to Christian youth about sexual purity

My Lord King

My Lord King
How can my love for You be perfected
What words can I utter
What deeds can I perform

My Lord King
My passions for You can be as white hot flames
Or they can be as warm embers
But never do they go out

My Lord King
What songs can be sung to ably declare
The perpetual and enduring love
That grows with each passing moment

My Lord King
I stay prostrate before You in total worship
You are my one true idol
My hero and my captor

My Lord King
Though not having seen You
The sweet perfume of Your presence
Lingers after we have parted

My Lord King
Warrior, Shepherd, Master of my fate, Captain of my soul
What more can I give to You
Oh take it all, for I trust Your love

Mirrors Of Beauty

She looked into her mirror
And beheld a maiden fair
With meek and quiet spirit
Loved by God 'twas very clear

She kept on looking and did see
Much virtue shining through
And wondered was that vision her
A sister, loved so very dear

She walked along a quiet path
To waters clear and clean
And looked into its mirrors
Rippling soft with truths then seen

She wears a robe of righteousness
She's clad with Christ-like mind
A tender heart now beats within
Compassionate and kind

God's mirror-waters help her see
What beauties lie within
Reflections of such beauty, rare
She's a flawless maid to Him

Elusive Love

The grandest them that's e'er been sung
A song of love through ages rung
Nor pen or scroll can ever tell
The Spirit-fruit in soft hearts swell

Poets, young and old still try
To write and sing and reason why
But through all ages it remains
Elusive to hate's deadly game

Though truth is hailed and wisdom's taught
True love cannot be sold or bought
Tempered by Creator God
It spans the earth that men have trod

This love that never will let go
Gently through pure hearts will flow
So strong yet tender, it will be
Engaging through eternity

A Long Dark Road

A long, dark road to Bethlehem town
Leading to safety sure
The angels would protect Him now
The Holy child so pure

A long, dark road to Bethlehem town
Mary and Joseph trod
In that humble city fair
Born was the Son of God

A long, dark road to Bethlehem town
Lighted by stars above
Did show the shepherds where to find
God's greatest gift of Love

A long, dark road to Bethlehem town
Leading the wise men brave
To baby Jesus whom God did send
A dying world to save

The long, dark road to Bethlehem town
That led to a manger bed
Would one day lead all men to God
Just as the prophets said

Gilead's Balm

Dear God above, if You are real
Is there not a balm to heal?
Physicians come from every site
But Gilead's balm can soothe my plight

You could have suffered long with me
But you ignored my desperate plea
You made no attempt to try again
My life shall sing its last refrain

Dear God I cry, I'm weary worn
Choose life or death, oh how I'm torn
This is the end; I'll call it quits
And to my head the pistol's fixed

The triggers pulled, the hammer jams
A voice says "Hear the Great I AM
I died so you would escape this
My plans for you are peace and bliss

I suddenly begin to rise
Toward the blue expanse of skies
The deliverer came and brought me out
I'm whole and free, there's no doubt

My feet now stand on solid ground
Unmoved, unshaken, now I've found
His words of love like honey sweet
His will, His work is now my meat

Angels Unaware

An angel walked into our hearts
One day quite unaware
Weaving threads of precious gold
With tender, loving care

A friendly smile adorned her face
So gentle, warm and bright
Beloved sister, loyal, true
In heart, both day and night

This fragrant flower, soft and sweet
Though gone, her scent still lingers
She's touching us from heaven above
With gentle, stroking fingers

This angel's gone, but sorely missed
But your presence here remains
We'll not forget your deeds of love
Our loss is heaven's gain

Dear friends and loved ones though you grieve
Your memories of me
Of moments shared, of laughter, tears
Will live eternally

A Mother's Love

A seed is planted in the womb
A mother's love is born
Never will its strength be broken
Nor from her heart be torn

A mother's love can never dwindle
Never will it fade
And though death bringer her parting sorrow
It lives beyond the grave

Mother dear, though grief and pain
Bring tears and lonely hours
Your mother-love will outlast
The bitter loss that's yours

Sweet memories from yesteryear
Bring healing to your heart
Remember your "love' is with the Lord
Don't let that thought depart

Tomorrow is another day
Hopes rise above the gloom
Take courage, for death's pain is o'er
And yours will end real soon

Prepared For War

Men of standard men of war
See your Lord has gone before
Keep the munitions, watch the way
Guard the city day by day

Fathers, brothers, young and old
Into slavery you were sold
But now you're free in heart and mind
To Satan's evils don't be blind

Make up the hedge, stand in the gap
Don't just sit with your hands in your lap
Repair the breaches, restore the ways
Build your futures till end of days

Men of honour, men of valour
Know this is your finest hour
The alarm has sounded, now take up the sword
The sword of the Spirit, God's Holy Word

You're armed for battle, do not fear
Jehovah Shammah, He is there
Fight the good fight with all your might
Win by faith, not by sight

Valiantly you've fought and won
Victorious men, through God's own Son
Back to back, shoulder to shoulder
A mighty force, you're stronger, bolder

Saved To Surrender

Amazing grace has set me free
Your love sustains me constantly
Where can I go, what can I do
I cannot make it without You

You met me in a sinful place
And saved me through Your matchless grace
You overlooked my sin and shame
And placed upon me Your great name

You sealed me for eternity
You placed in me Your destiny
You wrote Your will upon my heart
And called so gently to come apart

I'm standing now on holy ground
Because of You, my soul has found
Your purpose, with contentment sweet
In worship I bow and kiss Your feet

Dear Master I surrender all
To You, I'm at Your beck and call
Help me to hear and to obey
Your voice and follow You all the way

www.ingramcontent.com/pod-product-compliance
Ingram Content Group UK Ltd.
Pitfield, Milton Keynes, MK11 3LW, UK
UKHW041953230426
12048UKWH00008B/320